For Positive Change:

A Dhamma Talk
And Reflective Journal

Five Factors
For Positive Change:

A Dhamma Talk
And Reflective Journal

Bhanthe Sankichcha

EHIPASSIKO PRESS

Ehipassiko Press, LLC
Farmington Hills, Michigan

Ehipassiko: Encouraging Investigation

Ehipassiko Press

2023

Published August 2023

In the spirit of Open Educational Resources (OERs) and of not charging for the *dhamma*, we have priced the paperback edition of this book at cost of production. Neither the author nor publisher receive any royalties or other compensation for the sale of this book. Free .pdf files of the book are available online at ehipassikopress.org.

Cover Image:

The image on the cover combines a vertical cross section of the human brain that appeared in J.M. Bourgery and N.H.Jacob's *Traité complet de l'anatomie de l'homme,* vol. 3'(1844) with Claude Monet's *Water Lilies* (1916) in the brain cavity. The Buddha is from the Greco-Buddhist art of Gandhara (c. first century). A hand-colored photograph of a lotus created by Ogawa Kazumasa (1896) completes the piece.

CONTENTS

ACKNOWLEDGMENTS

Ehipassiko Press' business model has no income stream. Copies of our books are made available online for free. Paperback editions are sold through Amazon at cost of production. Neither our authors nor Ehipassiko Press receive any royalties or other compensation. All books are published at a financial loss. Therefore, we are especially grateful to the following individuals without whose contributions, this book would not have been published.

Bhanthe Sankichcha appreciates the conversations he had with Antonio Sieira about the relationship between therapeutic practices and Buddhism.

Jessica Worden-Jones served as editor.

Josselyn Moore served as copy editor.

Carson Sangala provided research assistance.

Illustrations were provided by the following individuals who released their photographs on Pixabay: 1195789, KIMDAEJEUNG, Lancier, ajs1980518, Victoria-Regen, 4753994, ElinaElina, and tenomgroup.

INTRODUCTION

Dhamma talks do not, typically, begin as a printed text which is read to the sangha, the community of believers. Instead, the monastic instructs devotees much like a teacher in a classroom instructs their students.

Five Factors for Positive Change, the second book in our "A Dhamma Talk and Reflective Journal Series," began as a presentation. Working with Bhante Sankichcha, volunteers transcribed and edited the talk and wrote the reflection questions. This is the same process used for our first book, *Learning from Others* and the one we intend to use for future publications in this series.

We "edit" the talk because literal transcripts do not typically translate well to a written text. But we edit lightly. We want to maintain the flavor of the spoken word and not lose the author's voice in the published version. Because they originated as talks and not manuscripts, I enjoyed reading *Five Factors for Positive Change* and *Learning from Others* out loud.

Reading out loud not only slowed me down so that I did not rush through Bhante Sanckichcha's enlightening words, but it also helped me capture the cadence of the talk as it was originally given. Reading out loud increased my enjoyment of the printed word.

A Note on Illustrations

This book has been illustrated with lotus flowers that have animals near them. The artists released their photographs on Pixabay under a license that is even more generous than the one we use for this series. We appreciate their generosity in allowing us to use their work for free.

The lotus flower is an appropriate illustration for change. It begins its life in the mud, in the negatives that Bhante Sankichcha discusses. Then it grows and changes into a beautiful flower. The images we selected include animals because Bhante Sankichcha has a special love for animals. In the first book of this series, *Learning from Others*, he includes a section on what we can learn from our pets and other animals found in nature.

Steven L. Berg, PhD
Publisher
Ehipassiko Press

Image Credit: 1195789

FIVE FACTORS FOR POSTIVE CHANGE

Five factors from Buddhist psychotherapy can be identified as practical techniques that you can apply to your mind, your behavior, your attitudes—basically to all your daily activities, especially to your spiritual practice and spiritual development.

Motivation

The first quality in this five-factor model is motivation. The motivation is the very best quality in this theory because everything has to begin with the motivation. Without motivation, we would not be able to create anything. Therefore, to have this refreshing motivation is very essential in the beginning and as we continue our practice, our journey.

Whether it is a spiritual practice or if it is any of your goals in life, you need to have that motivation always. Motivation really moves us forward. A lack of motivation will distract us. So, therefore, we need to make sure our motivation is in the right place, in the right direction.

Motivation has to be led by your right understanding because you can motivate yourself into wrongdoings, in the wrong directions. Your motivation must be shaped by your wisdom, your reasoning, your intellectual mind. Only then can your motivation take you to the desired goal, to a positive outcome.

For many people this motivation can be developed, a vision can be maintained, or motivation can be encouraged due to having your good friends around you. Good friends can always motivate us.

Sometimes our own life experiences can motivate us. We may get very heart touching and very sensitive or powerful life experiences. They can open up our mind. They can open up our eyes and help us begin to see the world from a totally different perspective. They can motivate us to do certain things, especially getting into a spiritual journey.

There can be many other things that can motivate us.

Identification

The second step is identification. Once you motivate yourself to reach somewhere, to achieve any goal, or to initiate something and continue, you should be able to identify certain things. These things are coming from two directions: distractions and supporting factors.

Whenever you want to achieve something, whenever you want to move forward, there are always going to be distractions, negative conditions in your way. So, we have to be mindful of these distractions and other disturbances. We need to ask, "What can take me down? Weaken my practice? My sanity?" This kind of awareness, this sensitivity to our negative conditions and circumstances is important. Otherwise, we can easily get caught up in these negativities. There are dangers, of course, in the world, in society, and there are negative thoughts, feelings, and emotions. They are still in our minds. So, we have to be able to identify them.

Then, of course, we have to be able to identify what are the supportive factors. What are the good qualities, positive qualities? When you want to achieve something, achieve some goal, you need to identify what are the supporting factors. You need to know these factors to enhance those qualities, to make yourself strong in your journey, your practice.

We learned all these good things in dhamma, right? How to have spiritual friends. How to have confidence. How to have right effort, mindfulness, concentration. All these good qualities, like loving kindness, sharing, generosity, and patience are very supportive to our practice or whenever we wanted something. They are supportive for any goal. Because we have to identify these positive qualities, identification is very important as the second factor in this five-step process.

Elimination

The third step is elimination. We have to be able to let go of these negative conditions. We have to be smart in that. We have to be very skillful because that can be one of the most difficult tasks, a difficult challenge for us, for anyone.

Of course, there are going to be distractions. We have to be able to let go of these negative conditions, what we identify in meditation practice as hindrances. Somehow, we have to learn how to let go. We have to be very skillful in doing that. And that's not easy either because most of the time, our mind—our human tendency—is to sometimes enjoy these negativities. Our corrupted mind, our unskillful mind, always finds indulgence in some negativities, like how one can enjoy one's own anger. It's the result of a corrupted mind, a deluded mind.

There are moments like that in all of us, so many different ways we enjoy our negativities. Even though they are negative, we don't see that. We don't see how the negativities affect our behavior, our progress, our moving forward. Therefore, it is time for us to let go of these negativities.

The other reason that this step is difficult is because we have been carrying the negativities for a long time. For a long time, we have been having connections with these negativities. Therefore, it is very difficult to let go. They are kind of imprinted in our system, in our brain, in our wiring. Maybe that's why it's difficult to let go. Even though we want to, it's difficult to let go.

Most commonly, we can let go of our past. Our past memories are negative sometimes, yet we like to bring them into the present moment and enjoy them even though they are negative. That's the kind of pattern or habit in our mind, in our human behavior. Therefore, we have to be skilled and smart in letting go of these distractions, these negative conditions and influences, as they appear.

How can you be smart? As the negativities come in, sometimes we can replace them with positive qualities. For example, our anger can be replaced with loving kindness and compassion. We can replace the negative conditions, negative qualities with positive ones. As we learn in the dhamma, we need to suppress these negativities.

We should apply our effort not to express negativities, but to encourage positive qualities with good effort. We have to let them go.

There's another approach we can take. Sometimes Buddha says, "look away." Don't look at negativities even when they are present. That means that when they are present, we need to neglect them.

Whenever they are present in yourself forget about them, don't encourage them. That is another way to let go of negativities, just like you avoid looking at a bad person. You keep a distance. Just like that.

There are different steps, different guidelines to eliminate negativities. Although elimination is very important, at the same time, our practice would not be completed just by letting go.

Cultivation

The fourth step is cultivation. After the elimination, we have to cultivate the positive qualities. What are the supporting practices? What can motivate ourselves more? What can keep us engaged in the practice to reach our goals? We need to identify the necessary positive qualities and learn how to incorporate them, make them a part of our practice. That is the secret.

Going forward, we will maintain them in our practice by doing them every day. These kind of positive qualities were learned in the dhamma. All the positive qualities to spiritual and skillful means are supportive practice for us. We learn them in the dhamma as the five spiritual faculties:

1. *Saddha*, the faith that counters doubt.
2. *Viriya*, the energy and effort that counters laziness.
3. *Sati*, the mindfulness that counters thoughtlessness.
4. *Samādhi*, the concentration that counters distraction.
5. *Pañña*, the wisdom that counters ignorance.

We have the beauty of these to embody confidence, right effort, mindfulness, concentration and wisdom, loving kindness, compassion, patience. You know how to be gentle and kind to oneself and others, to have patience. You know the humbleness, especially the qualities learned in the

Metta Sutta. In the first part of the *Metta* Sutta, we learn to be easily satisfied and maintained, to be easily instructed.

> This is what should be done
>> By one who is skilled in goodness,
> And who knows the path of peace:
>> Let them be able and upright,
> Straightforward and gentle in speech,
>> Humble and not conceited,
> Contented and easily satisfied,
>> Unburdened with duties and frugal in
>> their ways.
> Peaceful and calm and wise and skillful,
>> Not proud or demanding in nature.
> Let them not do the slightest thing
>> That the wise would later reprove.
> Wishing: In gladness and in safety,
>> May all beings be at ease.

These kinds of positive qualities are very important, very supportive. They can become a life divine. They can make our journey comfortable and peaceful and enjoyable.

We must be very skillful in cultivating these necessary qualities as needed. Otherwise, just the prevention of negativities would not complete our journey.

Some people do not appreciate the need for cultivation. These people say, "Oh, I didn't do anything wrong." Or some people say, "I didn't do anything bad." That's not enough. Some people get satisfied just by saying that. But according to the dhamma, that would not be sufficient. That would not be enough to complete our journey. That would not take us anywhere.

Not doing anything wrong is a great protection indeed. It would be the foundation for us because the first step is to let go of the bad: *sabba-pāpassa akaraṇaṃ*, not to do any evil action. But to complete the journey, we must move to the second step, *kusalassa upasampadā*, which is to cultivate the goodness. We have to practice all the good, beautiful, positive things in our lives. That is necessary, that is indeed very essential. After elimination, we have to cultivate all these spiritual qualities.

This cultivation makes us different. It makes us highly developed and highly evolved in our human journey, in our human experience, in our spiritual practice. The cultivation is the most important part. And then comes the final step, which is the most difficult.

Maintenance

When we learn maintenance, we make positive practices consistent. We make them regular. We apply these things again and again, again and again, again and again. This is the way to maintain them.

Our mind is getting deluded. Our mind is getting impure. Our mind is getting all too disturbed and distracted again and again, repeatedly, repeatedly. That's why we need to apply these positive techniques, the positive cultivation part repeatedly as well.

If you let go one moment, that would be enough for your mind to get distracted and make the disastrous situation. That's how emotions, our mind, our attitudes are. In the dhamma, it is called a way of life. A way of life means this practice is not just for one hour, one day, one week, one year. No, it has to be there all the time, *Sadhu sato*. This is our goal, to live the dhamma every day, every single moment.

Even though it sounds like a big challenge, it can happen naturally once you learn to appreciate and enjoy the positive transformations. Then it becomes natural. You don't have to run after these things. Instead, these qualities will follow once you learn how to appreciate them, once you learn to enjoy them in your life. That is a way to make it more natural to you.

The maintenance is a very difficult part. One of the biggest challenges is not being able to see a clear transformation in our practice, in our life, because we lack that maintenance. Sometimes we neglect. We don't pay enough attention and appreciation to our duties. We do it here and there whenever we remember or whenever time is available.

Especially when we want to achieve something meaningful, we want to cultivate our spirituality. It has to be a part of our everyday life. That is what we call the maintenance.

There can be so many things, so many conditions to distract us and to weaken ourselves, to weaken our motivation and all of these necessary steps. So, we have to be very skillful in maintaining these five steps: motivation, identification, elimination, cultivation, and maintenance. These five factors are very essential.

Even in psychotherapy, in every single practice, they apply this model, so this can be a Buddhist way of psychotherapy if you apply these five steps to your own behavior, your own mind, your own character, your own behavior. So, these five steps are very essential as we move forward. These five essential steps can benefit your practice. They can benefit your everyday life.

Image Credit: KIMDAEJEUNG

QUESTIONS FOR INQUIRY

This book was designed as a journal with plenty of room to reflect on the questions in the book itself. Prompts are provided at the top of each of the following pages, prompts you can use or ignore.

Writing out our reflections can be important because the process of writing makes us more likely to be honest with ourselves.

Image Credit: Lancier

MOTIVATION

What are some of my goals?

What motivates me to pursue them?

What good friends motivate me? How?

What life experiences motivate me? How? Why?

Was there a specific life experience that helped motivate me on my spiritual journey?

Reflect on a situation where you lost your motivation. Ask yourself, "Why did it happen? What did I do about it?"

IDENTIFICATION

What are some restrictions that stand in the way of achieving my goals?

What are some negative conditions that interfere with reaching my goals?

What can take me down, cause me to give up on my pursuits?

What can weaken my spiritual or other practices?

What are things that negatively impact my sanity?
my mental health?

What are some of the negative thoughts, feelings, and emotions that are still in my mind?

In what ways does my mind get disturbed and distracted?

What are some of the supporting factors, the good qualities, or positive qualities that I have in my life?

How can I enhance those supportive, good, positive qualities?

How did I learn (or continue to practice) right effort, mindfulness, concentration?

How did I learn (or do I practice) such good qualities as loving kindness, sharing, generosity, and patience?

Image Credit: Victoria-Regen

ELIMINATION

How do I enjoy my own anger?

What are other negativities or hindrances that I enjoy?

What are ways that negativities and hindrances affect my behavior, my progress, my moving forward?

Think of a specific goal that you have. Then ask yourself "How do negativities and hindrances impede me on the path to accomplishing my goal?"

How do negativities and hindrances impede my
spiritual progress?

In what ways do I encourage the negativities and hindrances in my life?

What negativities and hindrances would it be better for me to neglect, to not pay attention to?

What good qualities could replace the negativities and hindrances that I identified?

What are steps I could take to walk away from my negativities and hindrances?

Image Credit: 4753994

CULTIVATION

What are some supporting practices I can develop? How will I go about developing them more?

What motivates me? How can I better practice these traits in my life?

What can keep me engaged in the practice of my goals?

How do I practice the five spiritual faculties: *saddha* (faith), *viriya* (energy/persistence), *sati* (mindfulness), *samādhi* (concentration), and *pañña* (wisdom)?

What can I do to better cultivate the five spiritual faculties in my life: *saddha* (faith), *viriya* (energy/persistence), *sati* (mindfulness), *samādhi* (concentration), and *pañña* (wisdom)?

What are some qualities that allow me to be easily satisfied and maintained? How do I cultivate them?

What are some qualities that allow me to be easily instructed? How do I cultivate them?

What brings me comfort, peace, and enjoyment? How can I cultivate these in my life?

Image Credit: ElinaElina

CULTIVATION OF THE *METTA SUTTA*

In what ways do I act with skillfulness and goodness?

In what ways am I noble and upright?

In what ways am I straightforward and gentle in my speech?

In what ways am I contented, easily satisfied, unburdened with duties, and frugal in my ways?

In what ways am I peaceful and calm and wise and skillful?

In what ways am I not proud or demanding in nature?

In what ways do I not do the slightest thing that the wise would later reprove?

In what ways do I act in ways that demonstrate that I wish, in gladness and in safety, that all beings may be at ease?

Image Credit: tenomgroup

MAINTAINANCE

What do I do to live the dhamma every year? For example, are there special things that I do once a year such as attend the Vesak ceremony[1] or a retreat?

---

[1] Vesak is celebrated each May. Theravada Buddhists believe that the full moon day in May is the anniversary of Siddhartha Gautama, his enlightenment when he became the Gautama Buddha, and his death.

[s[sic]

[sic][sic][sic][sic][sic][sic][sic][sic][sic][sic][sic][sic][sic][sic][sic][sic][sic][sic][sic][sic][sic][sic][sic][sic][sic][sic][sic][sic][sic][sic][sic][sic][sic][sic][sic][sic][sic][sic][sic][sic][sic][sic][sic][sic]

What do I do to live the dhamma every month? For example, are there special things that I do once a month such attend a Poya day[2]?

[2] Poya days are held in conjunction with the full moon. Buddhists go to temple on Poya days for meditation, dhamma talks, and instruction.

What do I do to live the dhamma every week? For example, are there special things that I do once a week such as attend a meditation class or meet with dhamma or other learned friends?

What do I do to live the dhamma every day? For example, do I meditate, chant the Five Precepts,[3] or stay in contact with dhamma friends?

---

[3] The five precepts are to refrain from taking life, to refrain from taking what is not freely given, to refrain from sexual misconduct, to refrain from speaking falsely, and refrain from the use of intoxicants.

In what other ways do I make my dhamma practice a way of life?

What do I do on a yearly, monthly, weekly basis to obtain my other, non-spiritual goals?

What do I do on a daily basis to obtain my other, non-spiritual goals?

.

ABOUT EHIPASSIKO PRESS

Ehipassiko: Encouraging Understanding

Ehipassiko Press, LLC was started in June 2023 to publish Open Educational Resources (OERs) primarily in the fields of education, spirituality, and addiction recovery. Although not all our publications are Buddhist, we extend the Buddhist tradition of not selling Dhamma to all our books. Therefore, our books are published with a Creative Commons license and are released online for free.

In the spirit of OERs and not selling Dhamma, paperback editions of our books are offered through Amazon for cost of production. Neither our authors nor Ehipassiko Press receive royalties or other forms of compensation.

Please go to ehipassikopress.org for information about our other publications.

You may contact us at info@ehipassikopress.org.

GLBV | Center for Inner Peace & Meditation

ABOUT
GREAT LAKES BUDHIST VIHARA

The Great Lakes Buddhist Vihara (GLBV) is a Buddhist Monastery in the Theravada tradition, established in 1997 in the suburban Detroit area. GLBV provides services to the Great Lakes region, namely Michigan, Ohio, Indiana, and Ontario. Even though that Vihara is modeled after a typical Sri Lankan temple and run by Buddhist monks who are trained and ordained in Sri Lanka, the GLBV is for all who like to learn and practice Buddhism and meditation.

The GLBV provides free meditation classes, monthly Sil Days and other activities.

The GLBV is a 501(c)(3) non-profit organization.

ABOUT THE AUTHOR

Bhante Sankichcha was born in Kandy, Sri Lanka in 1976. In 1991, at the age of 15, he entered the monastic life at Sri Subodhārāma International Monks' Training Institute in Kandy.

In 1996 Bhante Sankichcha received his higher ordination (upasampadā). The same year, he moved to Australia where he lived for four years conducting numerous mindfulness programs. In 2001, he was invited to the Great Lakes Buddhist Vihara in Michigan, United States of America to continue his Dhamma services. He currently serves as the abbot of Great Lakes Buddhist Vihara.

Bhante Sankichcha received his BA degree in Psychology from Wayne State University in Detroit, Michigan. He is currently enrolled in a master's degree in counseling psychology program at Oakland University.

He is engaged in many social and religious services both locally and internationally. As a meditation and Dhamma teacher, Bhathe Sankichcha provides Buddhist spiritual counseling to many people including young people and adults.

He has taught meditation and the Dhamma in Malaysia, Singapore, Australia, Canada, and the United States of America.

ADDITIONAL NOTES
AND REFLECTIONS

A Dhamma Talk
and Reflective Journal Series

Learning From Others (July 2023)
   by Bhante Sankichcha

Five Factors for Positive Growth (August 2023)
   by Bhante Sankichcha